Celebrate Love

A Romantic Collection of Wedding Day Quotes

Edited by
June Eding

hatherleigh
Improve your life. Change your world.

Hatherleigh Press is committed to preserving and protecting the natural resources of the earth. Environmentally responsible and sustainable practices are embraced within the company's mission statement.

Visit us at www.hatherleighpress.com and register online for free offers, discounts, special events, and more.

Celebrate Love
Text Copyright © 2017 Hatherleigh Press

Library of Congress Cataloging-in-Publication Data is available.
ISBN: 978-1-57826-660-9

Printed in the United States
10 9 8 7 6 5 4 3 2 1

CONTENTS

INTRODUCTION

A wedding marks an important passage as the day a couple embarks upon the journey of life together. With family and friends there to witness, a wedding is also a celebration of love in all its forms and the way love shapes who we are over a lifetime.

This book is made up of thoughts from poets, artists, philosophers, and even presidents on the nature of love, the meaning of marriage, the essence of life, and more. These words are organized into sections that reflect many of the moments and emotions experienced on the wedding day. The first section, **Love: The Gift of Romance and Love's Enduring Power,** features wise words on the nature of love. **New Adventures: Life Passages and the Excitement of New Journeys** includes thoughts on the new life that awaits a couple. **Partnership: Building a Strong Togetherness** explores how each person contributes to a strong relationship, and why working together as a team is at the core of a successful partnership. **Friends and Family: Treasured Bonds and the Roots of Love** honors the powerful impact of other people in our lives. **Remembrance: Honoring Memories of Loved Ones** provides an opportunity to honor the memories of those who have passed away or can't be present for the marriage. Lastly, **Celebration: Rejoicing in the Gift of the Wedding Day** provides quotes to help a couple appreciate the gift of the wedding day, even as it rushes by.

Whether these quotes offer a moment of meditation, inspire perspective, or help ignite a feeling of pure joy, use the words on these pages to bring a new layer of meaning to the wedding day and the days leading up to it for you and your partner.

LOVE

The Gift of

Romance

and Love's

Enduring

Power

Love colors all stages of our lives. For a couple, romance is an important part of a partnership. But love comes in other forms, too. Over the years, the love in a couple's lives grows with them as they face new challenges. These words may resonate with your feelings for your partner or another loved one in your life.

Life is the flower for which love is the honey.

VICTOR HUGO

❧

Love is cheering and sharing and compassion and giving and receiving. Love is an action thing more than a word thing, that brings comfort or joy or relief to anyone or anything.

ZIGGY MARLEY

❧

Love is composed of a single soul inhabiting two bodies.

ARISTOTLE

I love you without knowing how, or when, or from
where. I love you simply, without problems or pride:
I love you in this way because I do not know any
other way of loving but this, in which there is no I
or you, so intimate that your hand upon my chest
is my hand, so intimate then when I fall asleep your
eyes close.

PABLO NERUDA

૭૭

The art of love is largely the art of persistence.

ALBERT ELLIS

૭૭

The garden of love is green without limit and yields many fruits other than sorrow or joy. Love is beyond either condition: without spring, without autumn, it is always fresh.

RUMI

૭૨

In our life there is a single color, as on an artist's palette, which provides the meaning of life and art. It is the color of love.

MARC CHAGALL

૭૨

Love recognizes no barriers. It jumps hurdles, leaps fences, penetrates walls to arrive at its destination full of hope.

MAYA ANGELOU

༖

Love takes off masks that we fear we cannot live without and know we cannot live within.

JAMES BALDWIN

༖

You know you're in love when you don't want to fall asleep because reality is finally better than your dreams.

DR. SEUSS

If I had a flower for every time I thought of you...I could walk through my garden forever.

ALFRED TENNYSON

Love many things, for therein lies the true strength, and whosoever loves much performs much, and can accomplish much, and what is done in love is done well.

VINCENT VAN GOGH

We are most alive when we're in love.

JOHN UPDIKE

When you realize you want to spend the rest of
your life with somebody, you want the rest of your
life to start as soon as possible.

NORA EPHRON

❧

All you need is love. But a little chocolate now and
then doesn't hurt.

CHARLES SCHULZ

❧

Love is the emblem of eternity; it confounds all
notion of time; effaces all memory of a beginning,
all fear of an end.

GERMAINE DE STAEL

I love you because the entire universe conspired to help me find you.

PAULO COELHO

♡♡

If I know what love is, it is because of you.

HERMAN HESSE

♡♡

You don't love someone for their looks, or their clothes, or for their fancy car, but because they sing a song only you can hear.

OSCAR WILDE

♡♡

Morning without you is a dwindled dawn.

EMILY DICKINSON

♡♡

Of all the music that reached farthest into heaven, it is the beating of a loving heart.

HENRY WARD BEECHER

♡♡

Can you imagine how much I love you? The more I see you as years go by I know the only one for me can only be you My arms won't free you, my heart won't try.

HARRY WARREN

♡♡

What is love? It is the morning and the evening star.

SINCLAIR LEWIS

૭૭

Whatever our souls are made of, his and mine are the same.

EMILY BRONTË

૭૭

To be fully seen by somebody, then, and be loved anyhow—this is a human offering that can border on miraculous.

ELIZABETH GILBERT

૭૭

I am in you and you in me, mutual in divine love.

WILLIAM BLAKE

♥♥

I give you my love, more precious than money,
I give you myself, before preaching or law;
Will you give me yourself?

WALT WHITMAN

♥♥

Love is the flower you've got to let grow.

JOHN LENNON

♥♥

There is no remedy for love but to love more.

HENRY DAVID THOREAU

♥♥

Love is the beauty of the soul.

SAINT AUGUSTINE

♥♥

Love is but the discovery of ourselves in others, and the delight in the recognition.

ALEXANDER SMITH

♥♥

The secret of a happy marriage is finding the right person. You know they're right if you love to be with them all the time.

JULIA CHILD

ღ

There is only one happiness in this life, to love and be loved.

GEORGE SAND

ღ

Love is the joy of the good, the wonder of the wise, the amazement of the Gods.

PLATO

ღ

Love to faults is always blind, always is to joy inclined. Lawless, winged, and unconfined, and breaks all chains from every mind.

WILLIAM BLAKE

ᦕ

Your task is not to seek for love, but merely to seek and find all the barriers within yourself that you have built against it.

RUMI

ᦕ

I encountered in the street, a very poor young man who was in love. His hat was old, his coat was worn, his elbows were in holes; the water trickled through his shoes, and the stars through his soul.

VICTOR HUGO

♡

Love is the greatest refreshment in life.

PABLO PICASSO

♡

Love never gives up, never loses faith, is always hopeful, and endures through every circumstance.

I CORINTHIANS 13:7

ॐ

Love each other dearly always. There is scarcely anything else in the world but that: to love one another.

VICTOR HUGO

NEW ADVENTURES

Life Passages

and the

Excitement

of

New Journeys

Love takes us on many new adventures and makes us brave in ways we never thought possible. Here are some words to help you reflect on the adventures you have had as a couple and the new journeys that lie ahead. When things seem challenging, turn to the blessing of each others' love for strength, and remember what matters most.

We love because it's the only true adventure.

NIKKI GIOVANNI

꙳

A journey is like marriage. The certain way to be wrong is to think you control it.

JOHN STEINBECK

꙳

The purpose of life is to live it, to taste experience to the utmost, to reach out eagerly and without fear for newer and richer experience.

ELEANOR ROOSEVELT

꙳

What is that feeling when you're driving away from people and they recede on the plain 'til you see their specks dispersing? It's the too-huge world vaulting us, and it's good-bye. But we lean forward to the next crazy venture beneath the skies.

JACK KEROUAC, *On the Road*

❧

Never fear quarrels, but seek hazardous adventures.

ALEXANDRE DUMAS, *The Three Musketeers*

❧

Either life entails courage, or it ceases to be life.

E. M. FORSTER

❧

Come live with me, and be my love;
And we will all the pleasures prove
That valleys, groves, hills, and fields,
Woods or steepy mountain yields.

CHRISTOPHER MARLOWE

ço

Will you come travel with me?
Shall we stick by each other as long as we live?

WALT WHITMAN

ço

Those who prepared for all the emergencies of life
beforehand may equip themselves at the expense
of joy.

E. M. FORSTER

Love does not consist in gazing at each other, but in looking outward together in the same direction.

ANTOINE DE SAINT-EXUPERY

⚬⚬

He who loves, flies, runs, and rejoices; he is free and nothing holds him back.

HENRI MATISSE

⚬⚬

At the side of the everlasting why, is a yes, and a yes, and a yes.

E. M. FORSTER

⚬⚬

In the end, it's not the years in your life that count. It's the life in your years.

ABRAHAM LINCOLN

♡♡

Life is not a problem to be solved, but a reality to be experienced.

SØREN KIERKEGAARD

♡♡

The good life is one inspired by love and guided by knowledge.

BERTRAND RUSSELL

♡♡

He who has a why to live can bear almost any how.

FRIEDRICH NIETZSCHE

❧

If you love life, don't waste time, for time is what life is made up of.

BRUCE LEE

❧

Life itself is the most wonderful fairy tale.

HANS CHRISTIAN ANDERSEN

❧

How far you go in life depends on your being tender with the young, compassionate with the aged, sympathetic with the striving, and tolerant of the weak and strong. Because someday in your life you will have been all of these.

GEORGE WASHINGTON CARVER

♍

Life is a lot like jazz…it's best when you improvise.

GEORGE GERSHWIN

♍

Life is what we make it, always has been, always will be.

GRANDMA MOSES

Maybe that's what life is…a wink of the eye and winking stars.

JACK KEROUAC

We must be willing to let go of the life we have planned, so as to have the life that is waiting for us.

E. M. FORSTER

The chief danger in life is that you may take too many precautions.

ALFRED ADLER

Life is not an exact science, it is an art.

SAMUEL BUTLER

♡

Life becomes harder for us when we live for others, but it also becomes richer and happier.

ALBERT SCHWEITZER

♡

Let life happen to you. Believe me: life is in the right, always.

RAINER MARIA RILKE

♡

We must build dikes of courage to hold back the flood of fear.

MARTIN LUTHER KING, JR.

&

God gave us the gift of life; it is up to us to give ourselves the gift of living well.

VOLTAIRE

&

You're going to go through tough times—that's life. But I say, "Nothing happens to you, it happens for you." See the positive in negative events.

JOEL OSTEEN

&

Life is one big road with lots of signs. So when you riding through the ruts, don't complicate your mind. Flee from hate, mischief, and jealousy. Don't bury your thoughts, put your vision to reality. Wake Up and Live!

BOB MARLEY

ᛞ

Wherever you go, go with all your heart.

CONFUCIUS

ᛞ

Being deeply loved by someone gives you strength, while loving someone deeply gives you courage.

LAO TZU

We should all do what, in the long run, gives us joy, even if it is only picking grapes or sorting the laundry.

E. B. WHITE

ᏇᏇ

A sheltered life can be a daring life as well. For all serious daring starts from within.

EUDORA WELTY

ᏇᏇ

In rivers, the water that you touch is the last of what has passed and the first of that which comes; so with present time.

LEONARDO DA VINCI

When you rise in the morning, give thanks for the light, for your life, for your strength. Give thanks for your food and for the joy of living. If you see no reason to give thanks, the fault lies in yourself.

TECUMSEH

ϨϨ

PARTNERSHIP

Building a

Strong

Togetherness

Becoming a couple means union, but it also means allowing each person the room and space to grow on their own and live their own best life. Acting in the best interest of the relationship while maintaining independence requires compromise, and the ability to let go of expectations. Only then can a couple arrive at what being together really means.

The most empowering relationships are those
in which each partner lifts the other to a higher
possession of their own being.

PIERRE TEILHARD DE CHARDIN

♥♥

Love is what you've been through with somebody.

JAMES THURBER

♥♥

When you make the sacrifice in marriage, you're
sacrificing not to each other but to unity in a
relationship.

JOSEPH CAMPBELL

♥♥

Sensual pleasures have the fleeting brilliance of a comet; a happy marriage has the tranquility of a lovely sunset.

ANN LANDERS

♕

Once the realization is accepted that even between the closest human beings infinite distances continue, a wonderful living side by side can grow, if they succeed in loving the distance between them which makes it possible for each to see the other whole against the sky.

RAINER MARIA RILKE

♕

Love does not dominate; it cultivates.

JOHANN WOLFGANG VON GOETHE

A successful marriage requires falling in love many times, always with the same person.

MIGNON McLAUGHLIN

༼༽

Love is friendship that has caught fire. It is quiet understanding, mutual confidence, sharing, and forgiving. It is loyalty through good and bad times. It settles for less than perfection and makes allowances for human weaknesses.

ANN LANDERS

༼༽

I love you, not only for what you are, but for what I am when I am with you.

ELIZABETH BARRETT BROWNING

Immature love says: "I love you because I need you."
Mature love says: "I need you because I love you."

ERICH FROMM

❦

For where thou art, there is the world itself, and
where though art not, desolation.

WILLIAM SHAKESPEARE

❦

There are a hundred paths through the world that
are easier than loving. But who wants easier?

MARY OLIVER

❦

Don't smother each other. No one can grow in the shade.

LEO BUSCAGLIA

ço

A happy marriage is a long conversation which always seems too short.

ANDRE MAUROIS

ço

Have a heart that never hardens, and a temper that never tires, and a touch that never hurts.

CHARLES DICKENS

ço

All the beautiful sentiments in the world weigh less than a single lovely action.

JAMES RUSSELL LOWELL

૭૭

Let us always meet each other with [a] smile, for the smile is the beginning of love.

MOTHER TERESA

૭૭

Blessed is the influence of one true, loving human soul on another.

GEORGE ELIOT

૭૭

All married couples should learn the art of battle
as they should learn the art of making love. Good
battle is objective and honest—never vicious or
cruel. Good battle is healthy and constructive,
and brings to a marriage the principles of equal
partnership.

ANN LANDERS

❧

Love and compassion are necessities, not luxuries.
Without them humanity cannot survive.

DALAI LAMA

❧

The less routine the more life.

AMOS BRONSON ALCOTT

What do we live for, if not to make life less difficult for each other?

GEORGE ELIOT

❦

Life appears to me too short to be spent in nursing animosity, or registering wrongs.

CHARLOTTE BRONTË

❦

Life is far too important a thing ever to talk seriously about.

OSCAR WILDE

❦

Life is a succession of moments, to live each one is to succeed.

CORITA KENT

♡♡

Coming together is a beginning; keeping together is progress; working together is success.

HENRY FORD

♡♡

Alone we can do so little; together we can do so much.

HELEN KELLER

♡♡

Together we can face any challenges as deep as the ocean and as high as the sky.

SONIA GANDHI

ᏯᎮ

Don't worry about the world coming to an end today. It is already tomorrow in Australia.

CHARLES M. SCHULZ

ᏯᎮ

When love and skill work together, expect a masterpiece.

JOHN RUSKIN

ᏯᎮ

Love is being stupid together.

PAUL VALERY

ᏬᏇ

For happiness one needs security, but joy can spring like a flower even from the cliffs of despair.

ANNE MORROW LINDBERGH

ᏬᏇ

A dream you dream alone is only a dream. A dream you dream together is reality.

YOKO ONO

ᏬᏇ

The more one judges, the less one loves.

HONORÉ DE BALZAC

ҩ

Love doesn't just sit there, like a stone, it has to be made, like bread; remade all the time, made new.

URSULA K. LE GUIN, *THE LATHE OF HEAVEN*

ҩ

Affection is responsible for nine-tenths of whatever solid and durable happiness there is in our lives.

C. S. LEWIS

ҩ

FRIENDS AND FAMILY

Treasured Bonds

and the

Roots of Love

Every person has their own unique story of life and love, one that began long before he or she met their intended groom or bride-to-be. Being surrounded by those who helped us find ourselves first, so we could then find our partner, is a meaningful part of the wedding celebration. When a couple celebrates with family and friends, the joy they experience is reflected back to them in the faces of the people they love, and their love is magnified a hundredfold.

There is nothing on this earth more to be prized than true friendship.

THOMAS AQUINAS

Ꮙᎇ

The family is one of nature's masterpieces.

GEORGE SANTAYANA

Ꮙᎇ

Let us be grateful to people who make us happy, they are the charming gardeners who make our souls blossom.

MARCEL PROUST

Ꮙᎇ

Love is a friendship set to music.

JOSEPH CAMPBELL

९९

The bond that links your true family is not one of blood, but of respect and joy in each other's life.

RICHARD BACH

९९

Lots of people want to ride with you in the limo, but what you want is someone who will take the bus with you when the limo breaks down.

OPRAH WINFREY

९९

You don't choose your family. They are God's gift to you, as you are to them.

DESMOND TUTU

♥♥

One of the most beautiful qualities of true friendship is to understand and to be understood.

SENECA

♥♥

For there is no friend like a sister in calm or stormy weather; to cheer one on the tedious way, to fetch one if one goes astray, to lift one if one totters down, to strengthen whilst one stands.

CHRISTINA ROSSETTI

It is one of the blessings of old friends that you can afford to be stupid with them.

RALPH WALDO EMERSON

♧

Love is the crowning grace of humanity, the holiest right of the soul, the golden link which binds us to duty and truth, the redeeming principle that chiefly reconciles the heart to life, and is prophetic of eternal good.

PETRARCH

♧

Love is blind; friendship closes its eyes.

FRIEDRICH NIETZSCHE

In every conceivable manner, the family is link to our past, bridge to our future.

ALEX HALEY

۶۶

Don't walk behind me; I may not lead. Don't walk in front of me; I may not follow. Just walk beside me and be my friend.

ALBERT CAMUS

۶۶

The crown of these
Is made of love and friendship, and sits high
Upon the forehead of humanity.

JOHN KEATS

Friendship at first sight, like love at first sight, is said to be the only truth.

HERMAN MELVILLE

୧୨

A man's growth is seen in the successive choirs of his friends.

RALPH WALDO EMERSON

୧୨

My friends are my estate.

EMILY DICKINSON

୧୨

It seems to me that trying to live without friends is like milking a bear to get cream for your morning coffee. It is a whole lot of trouble, and then not worth much after you get it.

Zora Neale Hurston

We must take care of our families wherever we find them.

Elizabeth Gilbert

I always felt that the great high privilege, relief, and comfort of friendship was that one had to explain nothing.

Katherine Mansfield

A friend may well be reckoned the masterpiece of nature.

RALPH WALDO EMERSON

૭૭

One of the signs of passing youth is the birth of a sense of fellowship with other human beings as we take our place among them.

VIRGINIA WOOLF

૭૭

One's friends are that part of the human race with which one can be human.

GEORGE SANTAYANA

૭૭

The greatest sweetener of human life is Friendship. To raise this to the highest pitch of enjoyment, is a secret which but few discover.

JOSEPH ADDISON

❧

Each friend represents a world in us, a world not born until they arrive, and it is only by this meeting that a new world is born.

ANAÏS NIN

❧

Families are like fudge—mostly sweet with a few nuts.

AUTHOR UNKNOWN

It is not so much our friends' help that helps us, as the confidence of their help.

EPICURUS

৫৭

The love of family and the admiration of friends is much more important than wealth and privilege.

CHARLES KURALT

৫৭

But friendship is precious, not only in the shade, but in the sunshine of life, and thanks to a benevolent arrangement the greater part of life is sunshine.

THOMAS JEFFERSON

৫৭

A man's friendships are one of the best measures of his worth.

CHARLES DARWIN

❧

Accept the things to which fate binds you, and love the people with whom fate brings you together, but do so with all your heart.

MARCUS AURELIUS

❧

Of all possessions a friend is the most precious.

HERODOTUS

❧

But friendship is the breathing rose, with sweets in every fold.

OLIVER WENDELL HOLMES, SR.

Friends...they cherish one another's hopes. They are kind to one another's dreams.

HENRY DAVID THOREAU

My best friend is the man who in wishing me well wishes it for my sake.

ARISTOTLE

REMEMBRANCE

Honoring

the Memories

of

Loved Ones

A wedding day can feel bittersweet. Among the joy and happiness is often a feeling of sadness that certain people aren't there with us. Here are some quotes that can help provide you with an opportunity to honor the memories of those who have passed away or can't be present for the wedding. Choose those that are most meaningful to you; and, if it feels right, share the quote with your partner. These words can become part of the ceremony, a silent prayer, or even a moment of quiet reflection.

Remember with smiles and laughter.

LAURA INGALLS WILDER

୧୨

That though the radiance which was once so bright be now forever taken from my sight. Though nothing can bring back the hour of splendor in the grass, glory in the flower. We will grieve not, rather find strength in what remains behind.

WILLIAM WORDSWORTH

୧୨

What we have once enjoyed we can never lose. All that we love deeply becomes a part of us.

HELEN KELLER

Sweet is the memory of distant friends! Like the mellow rays of the departing sun, it falls tenderly, yet sadly, on the heart.

WASHINGTON IRVING

༄

Sorrow prepares you for joy. It violently sweeps everything out of your house, so that new joy can find space to enter. It shakes the yellow leaves from the bough of your heart, so that fresh, green leaves can grow in their place. It pulls up the rotten roots, so that new roots hidden beneath have room to grow. Whatever sorrow shakes from your heart, far better things will take their place.

RUMI

༄

There are dark shadows on the earth, but its lights are stronger in the contrast.

CHARLES DICKENS

❧

Where there is love there is life.

MAHATMA GANDHI

❧

It is love, not reason, that is stronger than death.

THOMAS MANN

❧

The deeper that sorrow carves into your being, the more joy you can contain. Is not the cup that holds your wine the very cup that was burned in the potter's oven? And is not the lute that soothes your spirit, the very wood that was hollowed with knives? When you are joyous, look deep into your heart and you shall find it is only that which has given you sorrow that is giving you joy. When you are sorrowful look again in your heart, and you shall see in truth that you are weeping for that which has been your delight.

KAHLIL GIBRAN

ॐ

The life of the dead is placed in the memory of the living.

MARCUS TULLIUS CICERO

ॐ

Fond Memory brings the light
Of other days around me.

THOMAS MOORE

ღ

Memory is the mother of all wisdom.

AESCHYLUS

ღ

So long as the memory of certain beloved friends
lives in my heart, I shall say that life is good.

HELEN KELLER

ღ

Memory is the treasury and guardian of all things.

MARCUS TULLIUS CICERO

♡♡

When you lose a loved one, you come to these crossroads. You can take the path that leads you down the aisle of sadness, or you can say, "I'm never going to let this person's memory die. I'm going to make sure everything they worked for continues."

BINDI IRWIN

♡♡

No memory is ever alone; it's at the end of a trail of memories.

LOUIS L'AMOUR

A thing of beauty is a joy forever:
Its loveliness increases; it will never
Pass into nothingness, but still will keep
A bower quiet for us, and a sleep
Full of sweet dreams, and health, and quiet
   breathing.

JOHN KEATS

ༀ

If in the twilight of memory we should meet once
more, we shall speak again together and you shall
sing to me a deeper song.

KAHLIL GIBRAN

ༀ

There is a sacredness in tears. They are not the
mark of weakness, but of power. They speak more
eloquently than ten thousand tongues. They are
the messengers of overwhelming grief, of deep
contrition, and of unspeakable love.

WASHINGTON IRVING

♡

Grief is in two parts. The first is loss. The second is
the remaking of life.

ANNE ROIPHE

♡

Loss and Possession, Death and Life are one.
There falls no shadow where there shines no sun.

HILAIRE BELLOC

I am going to notice the lights of the earth, the sun and the moon and the stars, the lights of our candles as we march, the lights with which spring teases us, the light that is already present.

ANNE LAMOTT

ꝗ

Old friends pass away, new friends appear. It is just like the days. An old day passes, a new day arrives. The important thing is to make it meaningful: a meaningful friend—or a meaningful day.

DALAI LAMA

ꝗ

Find a place inside where there's joy, and the joy will burn out the pain.

JOSEPH CAMPBELL

"Thank you" is the best prayer that anyone could say. I say that one a lot. Thank you expresses extreme gratitude, humility, understanding.

ALICE WALKER

꒰꒱

Ships that pass in the night, and speak each other in passing, only a signal shown, and a distant voice in the darkness; So on the ocean of life, we pass and speak one another, only a look and a voice, then darkness again and a silence.

HENRY WADSWORTH LONGFELLOW

꒰꒱

Joy's smile is much closer to tears than laughter.

VICTOR HUGO

If you transform [grief] into remembrance, then you're magnifying the person you lost and also giving something of that person to other people, so they can experience something of that person.

PATTI SMITH

♡

The days may come, the days may go,
But still the hands of memory weave
The blissful dreams of long ago.

GEORGE COOPER

♡

What greater thing is there for human souls than to feel that they are joined for life—to be with each other in silent unspeakable memories.

GEORGE ELIOT

CELEBRATION

Rejoicing

in the Gift

of the

Wedding Day

A wedding is the ultimate celebration of love and the many ways it enriches our lives. Sometimes, the day passes so fast and entails so much that it may be hard to grasp. These words will help you stay in the moment and appreciate the day—even if it isn't perfect. After all, your wedding day will only happen once. Take in as much of it as you can, and your beautiful memories will provide you with joy in remembering for years to come.

And remember: often times, it's the moments that aren't planned that delight us the most.

With an eye made quiet by the power of harmony, and the deep power of joy, we see into the life of things.

WILLIAM WORDSWORTH

ᕫᕫ

Let us celebrate the occasion with wine and sweet words.

PLAUTUS

ᕫᕫ

Don't cry because it's over, smile because it happened.

DR. SEUSS

ᕫᕫ

When you do things from your soul, you feel a river moving in you, a joy.

RUMI

᭣᭣

If we can just let go and trust that things will work out the way they're supposed to, without trying to control the outcome, then we can begin to enjoy the moment more fully. The joy of the freedom it brings becomes more pleasurable than the experience itself.

GOLDIE HAWN

᭣᭣

Joy is what happens to us when we allow ourselves to recognize how good things really are.

MARIANNE WILLIAMSON

Do not dwell in the past, do not dream of the future, concentrate the mind on the present moment.

BUDDHA

൭ഉ

Happiness, not in another place but this place…not for another hour, but this hour.

WALT WHITMAN

൭ഉ

Fan the sinking flame of hilarity with the wing of friendship; and pass the rosy wine.

CHARLES DICKENS

൭ഉ

In the sweetness of friendship let there be laughter, and sharing of pleasures. For in the dew of little things the heart finds its morning and is refreshed.

KAHLIL GIBRAN

♥

It is a fine seasoning for joy to think of those we love.

MOLIERE

♥

[A]ll who joy would win
Must share it,—Happiness was born a twin.

LORD BYRON

♥

Sometimes your joy is the source of your smile, but sometimes your smile can be the source of your joy.

THICH NHAT HANH

♈

Reflect upon your present blessings of which every man has many—not on your past misfortunes, of which all men have some.

CHARLES DICKENS

♈

That it will never come again is what makes life sweet.

EMILY DICKINSON

♈

Pay attention to the beauty surrounding you.

ANNE LAMOTT

ೞ

Be happy for this moment. This moment is your life.

OMAR KHAYYAM

ೞ

Beauty is whatever gives joy.

EDNA ST. VINCENT MILLAY

ೞ

The events in our lives happen in a sequence in time, but in their significance to ourselves they find their own order…the continuous thread of revelation.

EUDORA WELTY

ღ

I have drunken deep of joy,
And I will taste no other wine tonight.

PERCY BYSSHE SHELLEY

ღ

Rejoice with your family in the beautiful land of life!

ALBERT EINSTEIN